OPERATION SAFE SURROUNDINGS (OpSS)

::

THE EVIDENCE-BASED VIOLENCE PREVENTION STRATEGY

By

Joel M. Caplan

Leslie W. Kennedy

On Behalf Of

The Rutgers Center on Public Security

Issues in Spatial Analysis Series, Vol. 2

Edited by J. M. Caplan and L. W. Kennedy

2019

Newark, New Jersey

USA

Suggested Citation

Caplan, J. M. and Kennedy, L. W. (2019). *Issues in Spatial Analysis Series: Vol. 2. Operation Safe Surroundings: The Evidence-Based Violence Prevention Strategy.* Newark, NJ: Rutgers Center on Public Security.

Produced by the Rutgers Center on Public Security

Based at Rutgers University's School of Criminal Justice, the Rutgers Center on Public Security (RCPS) offers a multidisciplinary approach to the academic study and practical application of ways in which democratic societies can effectively address crime, terrorism and other threats to public security. This involves the prevention of, protection from and response to natural or man-made events that could endanger the safety or security of people or property in a given area. RCPS engages in innovative data analysis and information dissemination, including the use of GIS, for strategic decision-making and tactical action.

Visit www.rutgerscps.org

CONTENTS

Operation Safe Surroundings (OpSS)

CHAPTER 1

Maximizing Local Resources

Why Operation Safe Surroundings?

Enhance Public Safety with Existing Resources

Problem Statement

Violent crime is a problem and frequent cause for concern voiced by many constituents. Traditional person-oriented law enforcement responses to violent crime problems, focused on deterrence or incapacitation, raise many complex issues. A sole emphasis on law enforcement and other policing tactics to respond to violent crime spikes has mixed evidence of success and sustainability, and raises notable civil justice and public relations issues. Economic and social issues must also be considered when developing a comprehensive violence prevention strategy.

Policing *tactics* often shape violence prevention strategies and unduly raise expectations that the criminal justice system, alone, can solve crime problems. This inappropriately minimizes the burden and roles that multiple other stakeholders should play to mitigate chronic problems at risky places. Multiple resources need to be coordinated in optimal ways to respond to and reduce violent crime and to enhance public safety.

Local Needs

- Maximize existing resources to focus on places and people with the greatest needs in order to reduce crime and enhance public safety.
- Balance *policing* and *law enforcement* tactics with all other options.
- Establish an evidence-based strategy that is data-driven, transparent and sustainable.

Solution

Operation Safe Surroundings (OpSS) is a data-driven, transparent and sustainable strategy for crime prevention and risk mitigation through coordinated, multi-stakeholder, resource deployments that disrupt situational contexts of illegal behavior.

Operation Safe Surroundings establishes a forum and evidence-based process for problem-solving and tactical decision-making for responsive actions and follow-ups that enhance public safety via risk governance.

While law enforcement is commonly used as a synonym for policing, OpSS acknowledges that neither tactic is a comprehensive strategy for violence prevention, in and of itself. Therefore, OpSS makes clear distinctions among these concepts within the context of *public safety*, which refers more broadly to the general welfare and protection of the public from various dangers affecting people, property and collective well-being.

Policing, Law Enforcement and Public Safety

Policing can be both place-based and person-oriented, whereas law enforcement focuses only on people who violate the law. Public safety involves policing and law enforcement plus other tactics and resources.

- *Policing* encompasses a wide range of activities carried out by police officers to control the affairs of a community, especially with respect to maintenance of order, law, health, and safety.

Policing can be both place-based and person-oriented.

- *Law enforcement* is a key function of policing that refers specifically to enforcing the written rules governing society by discovering, deterring, stopping, and/or seizing <u>people</u> who violate the law.

- *Public safety* refers more broadly to the general welfare and protection of the public from various dangers affecting people, property, and collective well-being. Policing and law enforcement affect public safety; multiple tactics and stakeholders can enhance public safety. 'Safe surroundings' connotes the importance of reducing threats and risks within one's personal space through place-based strategies and tactics.

CHAPTER 2

Implementing OpSS

---

1. Convene an "OpSS Taskforce" comprised of key community stakeholders.

   a. At a minimum, this should include officials from most city departments and public safety programs already underway. Selected representatives of community agencies (e.g., NPOs) and local businesses may also be included.

   b. This often works best when spearheaded by a police chief, city mayor, or district attorney's/prosecutor's office.

2. Prioritize current problem issues (e.g., robbery; shootings; drugs; burglary; motor vehicle theft). OpSS can work for violent and property crimes, as well as other public safety threats.

3. Analyze spatial and temporal crime patterns with **Risk Terrain Modeling (RTM) to diagnose** environmental conditions that lead to these outcomes (e.g. vacant and abandoned properties).

4. Specify **risk narratives that connect** to the crime problem and add situational contexts, based on the risk factors identified by the risk terrain model(s).

    a. Note: risk narratives may change over time, compared to prior iterations of this step.

5. Prescribe **responsive actions to disrupt** the risk narratives. These may include new initiatives or policies, and/or the reallocation of existing resources (i.e., patrols, activities, programs) to places with the greatest needs.

6. Coordinate responsive actions and designate task managers to oversee them.

7. **Prioritize risky places** on a map and deploy resources
to these locations.

    a. Deployments should last approximately 30 days,
        with data collected about what actions were
        implemented, where, by whom, and at what
        levels of intensity.

    b. Coordinate and set expectations with community
        members and groups already working to address
        problems at priority places.

8. Re-convene the OpSS Taskforce every 4-6 weeks and
iterate steps 2-7 based on new analyses and
information.

    a. Crime patterns and risky places are likely to
        change in response to successful responsive
        actions. RTM analyses are sensitive to this and
        should be re-run accordingly.

    b. Prior to the next OpSS Taskforce meeting,
        analysts can evaluate outcomes from the
        responsive actions already completed, update

datasets, and diagnose new crime patterns with RTM to produce actionable reports for discussion.

    i. Use evaluations and reports to measure success and, as appropriate, to manage expectations and strengthen public relations.

c. Consider the following when evaluating outcomes:

    i. Changes to Relative Risk Values (RRVs) of targeted risk factors among pre/post risk terrain models.

    ii. Changes to the intensity of risk at places on the risk terrain maps (i.e., Relative Risk Scores of places over time)

    iii. Changes to crime counts/rates

iv. Predictive validity of risk terrain models, and your selected target areas.

d. Ground truth results as a way of determining progress in risk mitigation and improving surroundings. This can include soliciting community input, visiting sites for improvement, and collecting progress reports from agencies responsible for neighborhood improvement and upkeep.

Risk Terrain Modeling (RTM)

To Identify and Diagnose Risky Places

Risk Terrain Modeling (RTM) is an analytical technique that diagnoses environmental conditions that lead to crime (or other problems). It brings multiple sources of data together by connecting them to geographic places, then performs statistical calculations.

RTM adds situational contexts to data and forecasts new locations for crimes to emerge or persist. RTM is easily with RTMDx software from Rutgers University (rtmdx.com).

Risk Narratives

Stories that Connect to the Crime Problem

Risk narratives connect environmental features identified through RTM (e.g. see figure below) to the situational contexts for illegal behaviors that result in crimes at these places. Risk factors will likely differ for different crime types and across different cities, so risk narratives may differ too.

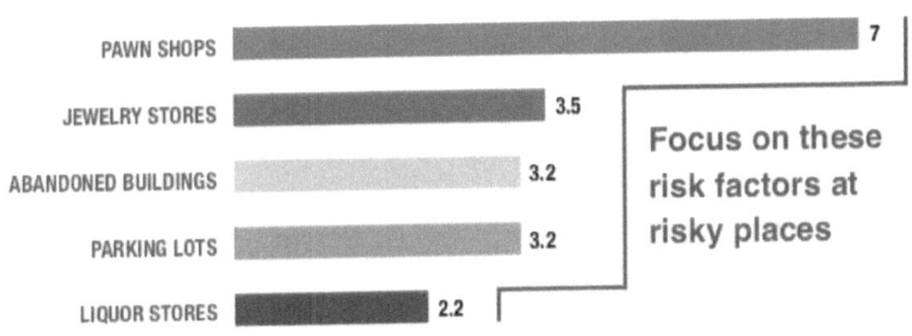

A risk narrative is a spoken or written account of places, people and behaviors that connect to crime problems at particular places. It considers dynamic interactions of people at places that can be understood (or hypothesized) and then disrupted.

Risk narratives offer an opportunity to solicit input from multiple perspectives and to add new meanings and contexts to analytical products.

For example, in one city, bodegas, vacant buildings and gas stations were diagnosed as risk factors for violent crime by the RTM. A community stakeholder explained how many youth hangout after school near corner stores/bodegas where they can easily congregate and get food, drinks, and items to smoke at nearby vacant buildings. Bodegas close at 10 p.m., as required by city ordinance, but gas stations with food marts are exempted. These 24-hour a day/7-day a week gas stations provide space and supplies for youth to congregate late at night, creating a unique context for turf conflict, offending, or victimization.

In another city, local residents complained about vacant properties that were used for illicit behaviors, but with so many vacant properties in the city, the task to address all of them was daunting. RTM objectively connected vacant properties to violent crime problems at particular places. This enabled city agencies to prioritize resources to board-up and secure vacant properties at the highest-risk places as a crime prevention tactic.

See also: riskterrainmodeling.com/situational-context.html

CHAPTER 4

Interventions Focused at Places

Disrupt Risk Narratives

Responsive Actions Focus on Key Factors at Risky Places

Risk narratives support reasoning with hypotheses, whereby preconceived notions about a crime problem and its relationships to space and time can be challenged, or clarified.

Because risk narratives articulate crime problems in diverse ways, multiple stakeholders can be engaged to solve crime problems, with multiple resources coordinated to address the key risk factors at priority places.

See also: riskterrainmodeling.com/risk-reduction.html

Risk Terrain Modeling (RTM) produces a map that 'paints a picture' of places where criminal behavior is statistically most likely to occur. Relative Risk Scores (RRSs) should be used to prioritize places on a risk terrain map (e.g., see figure below). Often, the places with RRSs greater than two standard deviations from the mean RRS are given priority.

Risk factors identified by RTM (i.e., in the tabular output) add transparency to risk terrain maps, and offer insights about what to focus on at high-risk places. This lets you prioritize crime prevention and risk reduction efforts at the target areas.

See also: riskterrainmodeling.com/maps--tables.html

CHAPTER 5
Evidence-Based Support for OpSS

Risk-Based Policing and RTM

Herman Goldstein published a seminal article in 1979 titled "Improving Policing: A Problem Oriented Approach." He argued that traditional policing suffered from a "means over ends syndrome". This results, he argued, in a reactive incident-based approach whereby police respond to crime events at the same places over time instead of solving recurring problems that encourage these crimes to emerge in the first place. Goldstein's thesis was a bold statement about the state of the policing profession, and it was a critical one that still resonates today.

Problem-Oriented Policing (POP) was conceived to improve the outcomes of policing activities by equipping officers with tools and information to solve the specific problems they dealt with in the line-of-duty (Goldstein, 2018). This requires data, analytics, skilled people, and a structured approach to using analytical outputs. This must support efforts to make informed decisions, deploy resources to the most problematic areas, and then systematically repeat these steps over time. It also requires resources and tactics beyond policing and law enforcement.

Sustainable and effective crime prevention strategies that also enhance public safety require: 1) identifying specific problems the public expects police to handle, 2) deeply understanding each problem, and 3) thinking creatively about the best possible "tailor-made" responses (Goldstein, 2018, p1).

Operation Safe Surroundings (OpSS) puts a high value on crime prevention efforts that do not depend solely on the criminal justice system but, rather, engage community stakeholders and other public and private resources to share the burden of public safety. It extends the principles of POP, building on the successes of risk-based policing (Kennedy, Caplan & Piza, 2018). Further, it offers a disciplined approach to crime prevention that encourages a multi-stakeholder focus on places to prevent crimes and mitigate crime risks. This approach has proven to be effective, and it is compatible with public demands and expectations for what a civilly just crime prevention strategy should be.

According to Kennedy, Caplan and Piza (2018), the five central tenets of risk-based policing are:

1) Focus on places, not only people, to prevent

crime;

2) Develop spatial risk narratives;

3) Solicit and value input from all ranks of police personnel and other community stakeholders about situational crime contexts, data management, expected outcomes, and performance measures;

4) Make data-driven decisions following a transparent process of problem definition, information gathering and analysis; and

5) Balance the real needs and expectations for *law enforcement* activities with comprehensive strategies for crime risk reduction and *public safety*.

Risk-based policing relies on the analytical framework provided by Risk Terrain Modeling (RTM). RTM is the product of over 40 years of systematic investigation, fieldwork and professional experience. It is based on scientific peer-reviewed research originating at Rutgers University and then replicated and published in the extant literature from around the world[1]. RTM has been used in over 45 countries across 6 continents and 35 states in the United States. It has a proven track record with successful outcomes that reflect community priorities.

In summary, RTM forecasts are better than predictions based on hot spot mapping. RTM outperforms methods used by 'predictive policing' apps. Directing police to high-risk places identified by RTM results in significantly lower crime. Risk terrain maps are easy to understand and to share with multiple stakeholders who need to know *where* to go and *why* to be there. Risk factors presented in tabular outputs add transparency to the maps. RTM is place-based, not person focused, so it is less susceptible to bias and it promotes positive engagements with communities.

Evaluations in multiple cities, funded by the U.S. Department of Justice, found that policing with RTM and targeting interventions at high-risk places, resulted in as much as 35% fewer gun crimes, 33% fewer motor vehicle thefts, and 42% fewer robberies, compared to control areas. And, there were many other positive outcomes

---

[1] A full bibliography of the research evidence is located at www.rtmworks.com

documented in all the jurisdictions studied. Focusing on risky places works to reduce violent and property crimes. RTM has also been applied to problem-solving efforts regarding drugs, traffic crashes, terrorism, homeland security and public health.

Place-Based Prevention

Place-based crime prevention rests on the notion that crimes emerge and spatially concentrate where there is something about the place that attracts illegal behaviors and leads to crime outcomes (Weisburd, 2008; Caplan & Kennedy, 2016). This presumption is well documented in research literature utilizing various methodologies including hot spot mapping (Haberman, 2017; Weisburd & Braga, 2006; Sherman, 1995; Sherman, Gartin, and Buerger, 1989; Schnell, Grossman, & Braga, 2018), near repeat analysis (Ratcliffe & McCullagh, 1998; Ratcliffe & Rengert, 2008; Johnson, 2008) and Risk Terrain Modeling (Caplan & Kennedy, 2016; Garnier, Caplan, and Kennedy, 2018; Connealy & Piza, 2019). It is also grounded in the Theory of Risky Places (Kennedy, Caplan, Piza, & Buccine-Schraeder, 2016), the Law of Crime Concentration (Weisburd, 2015),

Crime Pattern Theory (Brantingham & Brantingham, 1981), and other theoretical frameworks within the domain of criminology and criminal justice (e.g., Quetelet, 1984; Park, McKenzie & Burgess, 1925; Shaw & McKay, 1969; Brantingham & Brantingham, 1995).

By around 1970, ideas for crime prevention through environmental design (CPTED) emerged from within both the fields of criminology and architecture when researchers proposed that the physical environment often influences crime. Paul and Patricia Brantingham built from the cross-disciplinary ideas of CPTED to include more elements of the social environment and changed the focus to examine places and patterns of the events that occur in those places. They proposed that places exhibit physical features such as retail stores or entertainment venues that help provide criminal opportunities by bringing together offenders and targets in time and space. They (1995) explained that spatial crime patterns, and their stability over time, are a function of the 'environmental backcloth' of the area under study, which is dotted with "crime attractors" and "crime generators".

Kennedy, Caplan and Piza (2018) present data-informed justifications to focus on risks associated with certain types of environmental features at crime-prone areas. Certain features of the landscape exert spatial influences on human behaviors that can affect a place's vulnerability to crime – which is why crimes emerge, cluster and persist over time. Barnum, Caplan, Kennedy and Piza (2017), for example, demonstrated how, consistent with crime pattern theory (Brantingham & Brantingham, 1981) and the theory of risky places (Kennedy, Caplan, Piza & Buccine-Schraeder, 2016), the environmental backcloth affects how place features relate to and influence crime patterns. While it is theoretically and empirically evident that crimes cluster spatially, it is also clear that crime prevention efforts need to be tailored to specific environmental behavior settings in order to sufficiently cool crime hot spots and prevent their reemergence.

Operation Safe Surroundings (OpSS) is designed to offer clues on how to change situations to make them less conducive to crime and to focus less on law enforcement actions against people. Goldstein (2018) explains that law enforcement is commonly used as a synonym for policing, but enforcing the law is not the most sustainable response to the problems that police deal with regularly. OpSS reminds us that sustainable crime prevention strategies require more than only law enforcement tactics. Addressing the collective influences of environmental features that attract crime and generate illegal behavior-settings is needed for a crime prevention strategy that is place-based and not merely person-focused.

Utilizing RTM to analyze features of the environmental backcloth that aggravate crime risks offers city officials options for crime prevention that helps them target and mitigate risky features at priority places with all the various resources at their disposal. It offers an effective way to coordinate resources (Caplan & Kennedy, 2016; Kennedy, Caplan & Piza, 2018).

Police dealings with people at high crime areas may have the effect of deterring criminals or even reducing crime counts in the short-term. But, despite this, the underlying place-based factors that attract and generate problems in these areas do not go away. So, while the OpSS strategy accommodates the ideas of situational crime prevention (Guerette & Bowers, 2009; Clarke, 1997) in targeting certain locations for intervention, efforts can extend beyond a focus on opportunities for crime or the "crime triangle" (Cohen & Felson, 1979; Cohen, Kluegel, & Land, 1981). Instead, efforts can be made to target all aspects of the contexts that raise the risk of crime. OpSS enables a concerted effort by police plus other stakeholders to mitigate environmental attractors and generators that make particular areas suitable locations for crime time-and-again. OpSS disrupts the crime risk narratives to reduce crime and keep it low.

REFERENCES

Barnum, J. D., Caplan, J. M., Kennedy, L. W., & Piza, E. L. (2017). The Crime Kaleidoscope: A Cross-Jurisdictional Analysis of Place Features and Crime in Three Urban Environments. *Applied Geography, 79*, 203-211

Brantingham, P., & Brantingham, P. (1981). *Environmental criminology*. Beverly Hills, CA: Sage Publications.

Brantingham, P., & Brantingham, P. L. (1995). Criminality of Place: Crime Generators and Crime Attractors. *European Journal on Criminal Policy and Research 3*, 1-26.

Caplan, J. M. & Kennedy, L. W. (2016). *Risk Terrain Modeling: Crime Prediction and Risk Reduction.* Berkeley, CA: University of California Press.

Clarke, R. (1997). Introduction. In R. Clarke (Ed.), *Situational crime prevention, successful case studies* (2nd ed.). Monsey, NY: Criminal Justice Press.

Cohen, L. E., & Felson, M. (1979). Social change and crime rate trends: A routine activity approach. *American Sociological Review, 44*, 588-608.

Cohen, L., Kluegel, J., & Land, K. (1981). Social inequality and predatory criminal victimization: An exposition and test of a formal theory. *American Sociological Review, 46*(5), 505-524.

Connealy, N. T. & Piza, E. L. (2019). Risk Factor and High-Risk Place Variations Across Different Robbery Targets in Denver, Colorado. *Journal of Criminal Justice, 60*, 47-56.

Garnier, S., Caplan, J. M., & Kennedy, L. W. (2018). Predicting Dynamical Crime Distribution from Environmental and Social Influences. *Frontiers in Applied Mathematics and Statistics, 30.*

Goldstein, H. (2018). On Problem-Oriented Policing: The Stockholm Lecture. *Crime Science, 7(13)*, 1-9.

Guerette, R. T., & Bowers, K. J. (2009). Assessing the extent of crime displacement and diffusion of benefits: A review of situational crime prevention evaluations. *Criminology, 47*, 1331-1368.

Haberman, C. P. (2017). Overlapping Hot Spots? Examination of the Spatial Heterogeneity of Hot Spots of Different Crime Types. *Criminology & Public Policy, 16(2)*, 633-660.

Johnson, S. D. (2008). Repeat burglary victimization: A tale of two theories. *Journal of Experimental Criminology, 4*, 215-240.

Kennedy, L. W., Caplan, J. M., & Piza, E. L. (2018). *Risk-Based Policing: Evidence-Based Crime Prevention with Big Data and Spatial Analytics.* Berkeley, CA: University of California Press.

Kennedy, L. W., Caplan, J. M., Piza, E. L. & Buccine-Schraeder, H. (2016). Vulnerability and Exposure to Crime: Applying Risk Terrain Modeling to the Study of Assault in Chicago. *Applied Spatial Analysis and Policy. 9(4)*, 529-548.

Park, R. E., McKenzie, R. D., & Burgess, E. (1925). *The city: Suggestions for the study of human nature in the urban environment.* Chicago, IL: University of Chicago Press.

Quetelet, A. (1984). Research on the Propensity for Crime at Different Ages. (S.F. Sylvester, Trans.). Cincinnati, OH: Anderson Publishing. (Original work published 1831).

Ratcliffe, J. & Rengert, G. (2008). Near repeat patterns in Philadelphia shootings. *Security Journal, 21 (1-2)*: 58-76.

Ratcliffe, J. H., & McCullagh, M. J. (1998). Identifying repeat victimization with GIS. *British Journal of Criminology, 38*(4), 651-662.

Schnell, C., Grossman, L. & Braga, A. A. (2018, online first). The Routine Activities of Violent Crime Places: A Retrospective Case-Control Study of Crime Opportunities on Street Segments. *Journal of Criminal Justice.*

Shaw, C., & McKay, H. (1969). *Juvenile delinquency and urban areas.* Chicago, IL: University of Chicago Press.

Sherman, L. (1995). Hotspots of crime and criminal careers of places. In J. E. Eck & D. Weisburd (Eds.), *Crime and Place, vol. 4* (pp. 35-52). Monsey, NY: Criminal Justice Press.

Sherman, L. W., Gartin, P. R., & Buerger, M. E. (1989). Hot spots of predatory crime: Routine activities and the criminology of place. *Criminology, 27*, 27-56.

Weisburd, D., & Braga, A. A. (2006). Hotspots policing as a model for police innovation. In D. Weisburd & A. A. Braga (Eds.), *Police innovation: Contrasting perspectives* (pp. 225-244). New York, NY: Cambridge University Press.

* 9 7 8 1 0 8 7 1 0 8 0 1 8 *